# Richards

**by Iain Gray**

Lang**Syne**

**PUBLISHING**

WRITING *to* REMEMBER

# Lang**Syne**

**PUBLISHING**

WRITING *to* REMEMBER

79 Main Street, Newtongrange,
Midlothian EH22 4NA
Tel: 0131 344 0414   Fax: 0845 075 6085
E-mail: info@lang-syne.co.uk
www.langsyneshop.co.uk

Design by Dorothy Meikle
Printed by Ricoh Print Scotland
© Lang Syne Publishers Ltd 2015

ISBN 978-1-85217-671-6

# Richards

**MOTTO:**

With honour and love.

**CREST:**

A lion rampant.

**NAME** variations include:
Ricard
Richard
Rycard

*Chapter one:*

# Origins of Welsh surnames

by Iain Gray

**If you don't know where you came from, you won't know where you're going is a frequently quoted observation and one that has a particular resonance today when there has been a marked upsurge in interest in genealogy, with increasing numbers of people curious to trace their family roots.**

Main sources for genealogical research include census returns and official records of births, marriages and deaths – and the key to unlocking the detail they contain is obviously a family surname, one that has been 'inherited' and passed from generation to generation.

No matter our station in life, we all have a surname – but it was not until about the middle of the fourteenth century that the practice of being identified by a particular, or 'fixed', surname became commonly established throughout the British Isles.

Previous to this, it was normal for a person to be identified through the use of only a forename.

Wales, however, known in the Welsh language as *Cymru*, is uniquely different – with the use of what are known as patronymic names continuing well into the fifteenth century and, in remote rural areas, up until the early nineteenth century.

Patronymic names are ones where a son takes his father's forename, or Christian name, as his surname.

Examples of patronymic names throughout the British Isles include 'Johnson', indicating 'son of John', while specifically in Scotland 'son of' was denoted by the prefix Mc or Mac – with 'MacDonald', for example, meaning 'son of Donald.'

Early Welsh law, known as *Cyfraith Hywel*, *The Law of Hywel*, introduced by Hywel the Good, who ruled from Prestatyn to Pembroke between 915 AD and 950 AD, stipulated that a person's name should indicate their ancestry – the name in effect being a type of 'family tree.'

This required the prefixes *ap* or *ab* – derived from *mab*, meaning 'son of' being placed before the person's baptismal name.

In the case of females, the suffixes *verch* or *ferch*, sometimes shortened to *vch* or *vz* would be attached to their Christian name to indicate 'daughter of.'

In some cases, rather than being known for

example as *Llewellyn ap Thomas* – *Llewellyn son of Thomas* – Llewellyn's name would incorporate an 'ancestral tree' going back much earlier than his father.

One source gives the example of *Llewellyn ap Thomas ap Dafydd ap Evan ap Owen ap John* – meaning *Llewellyn son of Thomas son of Dafydd son of Evan son of Owen son of John*.

This leads to great confusion, to say the least, when trying to trace a person's ancestry back to a particular family – with many people having the forenames, for example, of Llewellyn, Thomas, Owen or John.

The first Act of Union between Wales and England that took place in 1536 during the reign of Henry VIII required that all Welsh names be registered in an Anglicised form – with *Hywel*, for example, becoming Howell, or Powell, and *Gruffydd* becoming Griffiths.

An early historical example of this concerns William ap John Thomas, standard bearer to Henry VIII, who became William Jones.

In many cases – as in Davies and Williams – an s was simply added to the original patronymic name, while in other cases the prefix *ap* or *ab* was contracted to *p* or *b* to prefix the name – as in *ab Evan* to form Bevan and *ap Richard* to form Pritchard.

Other original Welsh surnames – such as Morgan, originally *Morcant* – derive from ancient Celtic sources, while others stem from a person's physical characteristics – as in *Gwyn* or *Wynne* a nickname for someone with fair hair, *Gough* or *Gooch* denoting someone with red hair or a ruddy complexion, *Gethin* indicating swarthy or ugly and *Lloyd* someone with brown or grey hair.

With many popular surnames found today in Wales being based on popular Christian names such as John, this means that what is known as the 'stock' or 'pool' of names is comparatively small compared to that of common surnames found in England, Scotland and Ireland.

This explains why, in a typical Welsh village or town with many bearers of a particular name not necessarily being related, they were differentiated by being known, for example, as 'Jones the butcher', 'Jones the teacher' and 'Jones the grocer.'

Another common practice, dating from about the nineteenth century, was to differentiate among families of the same name by prefixing it with the mother's surname or hyphenating the name.

The history of the origins and development of Welsh surnames is inextricably bound up with the nation's frequently turbulent history and its rich culture.

Speaking a Celtic language known as Brythonic, which would gradually evolve into Welsh, the natives were subjected to Roman invasion in 48 AD, and in the following centuries to invasion by the Anglo-Saxons, Vikings and Normans.

Under England's ruthless and ambitious Edward I, the nation was fortified with castles between 1276 and 1295 to keep the 'rebellious' natives in check – but this did not prevent a series of bloody uprisings against English rule that included, most notably, Owain Glyndŵr's rebellion in 1400.

Politically united with England through the first Act of Union in 1536, becoming part of the Kingdom of Great Britain in 1707 and part of the United Kingdom in 1801, it was in 1999 that *Cynulliad Cenedlaethol Cymru*, the National Assembly for Wales, was officially opened by the Queen.

Welsh language and literature has flourished throughout the nation's long history.

In what is known as the Heroic Age, early Welsh poets include the late sixth century Taliesin and Aneirin, author of *Y Gododdin*.

Discovered in a thirteenth century manuscript but thought to date from anywhere between the seventh and eleventh centuries, it refers to the kingdom of Gododdin that took in south-east Scotland and

Northumberland and was part of what was once the Welsh territory known as *Hen Ogledd*, *The Old North*.

Commemorating Gododdin warriors who were killed in battle against the Angles of Bernicia and Deira at Catraith in about 600 AD, the manuscript – known as *Llyfr Aneirin*, *Book of Aneirin* – is now in the precious care of Cardiff City Library.

Other important early works by Welsh poets include the fourteenth century *Red Book of Hergest*, now held in the Bodleian Library, Oxford, and the *White Book of Rhydderch*, kept in the National Library of Wales, Aberystwyth.

William Morgan's translation of the Bible into Welsh in 1588 is hailed as having played an important role in the advancement of the Welsh language, while in 1885 Dan Isaac Davies founded the first Welsh language society.

It was in 1856 that Evan James and his son James James composed the rousing Welsh national anthem *Hen Wlad Fynhadad – Land of My Fathers*, while in the twentieth century the poet Dylan Thomas gained international fame and acclaim with poems such as *Under Milk Wood*.

The nation's proud cultural heritage is also celebrated through *Eisteddfod Genedlaethol Cymru*, the National Eisteddfod of Wales, the annual festival of music, literature and performance that is held across the nation and which traces its roots back to 1176 when Rhys ap Gruffyd, who ruled the territory of Deheubarth from 1155 to 1197, hosted a magnificent festival of poetry and song at his court in Cardigan.

The 2011 census for Wales unfortunately shows that the number of people able to speak the language has declined from 20.8% of the population of just under 3.1 million in 2001 to 19% – but overall the nation's proud culture, reflected in its surnames, still flourishes.

Many Welsh families proudly boast the heraldic device known as a Coat of Arms, as featured on our front cover.

The central motif of the Coat of Arms would originally have been what was borne on the shield of a warrior to distinguish himself from others on the battlefield.

Not featured on the Coat of Arms, but highlighted on page three, is the family motto and related crest – with the latter frequently different from the central motif.

Echoes of a far distant past can still be found in our surnames and they can be borne with pride in commemoration of our forebears.

*Chapter two:*

# Conquest and revolt

**A patronymic surname, with the final 's' denoting 'son of', 'Richards' is of martial roots in that it stems from the Germanic 'Ricard' – with 'ric' indicating 'power' and 'hard' indicating 'brave', 'hardy', or 'ruler.'**

The designation of 'ruler' is apt, because one of the reasons for the popularity of 'Richard' as a forename and from which the surname derives, is through admiration in medieval times for the twelfth century Richard I, Coeur de Lion – the Lionheart – who ruled as the English king from 1189 until his death at the age of 42 in 1199.

Famed for his role in the Third Crusade to the Holy Land from 1190 to 1192, it was on his return that he was seized and held to a hefty ransom by Leopold of Austria – whom he had somehow offended while the two monarchs were on crusade.

The name is identified from earliest times with South Wales, particularly in what is now the county of Glamorganshire, also known as Glamorgan, home to the Welsh capital of Cardiff and created through the *Laws of Wales Acts* of 1535 and 1542.

One of the thirteen historic counties of Wales and known in Welsh as *Sir Forgannwg* – with 'Sir' denoting county – it was originally the ancient kingdom known as Glywsing until it was usurped by the Normans.

It was the Norman Conquest of 1066 that sounded the death knell of not only Anglo-Saxon control of England but ultimately also of Welsh independence.

By this date, England had become a nation with several powerful competitors to the throne.

In what were extremely complex family, political and military machinations, the monarch was Harold II, who had succeeded to the throne following the death of Edward the Confessor.

But his right to the kingship was contested by two powerful competitors – his brother-in-law King Harold Hardrada of Norway, in alliance with Tostig, Harold II's brother, and Duke William II of Normandy.

On October 14, Harold II encountered a mighty invasion force led by Duke William that had landed at Hastings, in East Sussex.

He drew up a strong defensive position, at the top of Senlac Hill, building a shield wall to repel William's cavalry and infantry.

The Normans suffered heavy losses, but through a combination of the deadly skill of their archers and the ferocious determination of their cavalry they eventually won the day.

Morale had collapsed on the battlefield as word spread through the ranks that Harold had been killed, and amidst the carnage of the battlefield it was difficult to identify him.

Some sources assert William ordered his body to be thrown into the sea, while others state it was secretly buried at Waltham Abbey.

What is known with certainty, however, is that in celebration of his great victory William founded Battle Abbey, near the site of the battle, ordering that the altar be sited on the spot where Harold, the last of the Anglo-Saxon kings, was believed to have fallen.

William was declared King of England on December 25, and the complete subjugation of his Anglo-Saxon subjects followed, with those Normans who had fought on his behalf rewarded with lands – a pattern that would be repeated in Wales.

Invading across the Welsh Marches, the borderland between England and Wales, the Normans gradually consolidated gains by building castles – while under a succession of Welsh leaders who included Llywelyn ap Gruffudd, known as Llywelyn the Last, resistance proved strong.

But it was brutally crushed in 1283 under

England's ruthless and ambitious Edward I, who ordered the building or repair of at least 17 castles and in 1302 proclaimed his son and heir, the future Edward II, as Prince of Wales, a title known in Welsh as *Tywysog Cymru*.

A heroic Welsh figure arose from 1400 to 1415 in the form of Owain Glyndŵr – the last native Welshman to be recognised by his supporters as *Tywysog Cymru*.

In what is known as The Welsh Revolt he achieved an early series of stunning victories against Henry IV and his successor Henry V – until mysteriously disappearing from the historical record after mounting an ambush in Brecon.

Some sources assert that he was either killed in the ambush or died a short time afterwards from wounds he received – but there is a persistent tradition that he survived and lived thereafter in anonymity, protected by loyal followers.

During the revolt, he had consistently refused offers of a Royal Pardon and – despite offers of rewards for his capture – he was never betrayed.

Welsh bearers of the Richards name feature prominently in the colourful drama that is the historical record.

One particularly noteworthy family is the Richards of Betws Y Coed, in Dolgellau, Gwynedd.

Born in 1752, Sir Richard Richards was the judge and politician who served for a time in the powerful post of Baron of the Exchequer.

It was through his marriage in 1785 to Catherine Humphreys, daughter and heiress of Robert Vaughan Humphries, that he acquired the estate and mansion of Caerynwch, near Dolgellau, and which remains in the family to this day.

He died in 1823, while one of his sons, also named Richard Richards, served from 1836 until 1852 as Member of Parliament (MP) for Merioneth, while he also held the post of Account-General of the Court of Exchequer.

Born in 1787, he died in 1860, while his brothers Griffith Richards and Robert Richards were both appointed as Queen's Counsel and his sister Jane as Chaplain to the House of Commons.

*Chapter three:*

# Honours and distinction

**Bearers of the proud name of Richards have distinguished themselves through a colourful variety of endeavours and pursuits.**

Born in 1751 in Glanyrafon, near Bryn-crug, in Gwynedd, David Richards was the poet better known by his bardic name of Dafydd Ionwar.

A teacher from 1800 to 1807 in Dolgellau, after having penned Welsh language works that include his 1793 *Cywdd y Drinod* and his 1803 *Gwaith Prydyddawl*, he died in 1827.

In the twentieth century, Alun Morgan Richards was the novelist, former teacher and seaman whose acclaimed works include his 1977 *Ennal's Point*, the 1974 short story collection *Dai Country* and his 1980 *A Touch of Glory*, which marked the centenary of the Welsh Rugby Union; born in 1929 in Caerphilly, he died in 2004.

A noted scholar, Melville Grafton Richards was born in Ffair-fach, Carmarthenshire in 1910.

The son of a railway worker and having served in intelligence during the Second World War and later as head of the Celtic Studies Department at Liverpool

University, his many academic works include his 1954 *The Laws of Hywel Dda* and, seven years before his death in 1973, *Atlas of Anglesey*.

Striking a musical note, Henry Richards was the Welsh composer born in Carmarthen in 1871.

Musically gifted from an early age, he studied at the Royal Academy of Music before continuing his studies in Paris, where he was a pupil of Frederic Chopin.

Known by his bardic name of Pencerdd Towy, before his death in 1885 he had composed works that include his 1862 *God Bless the Prince of Wales*, written in honour of the future King Edward VII.

Known as the "Queen of the Harp", Nansi Richards Jones was the Welsh harpist recognised as having been a leading expert on both the pedal harp and the triple harp.

Born in 1888 in, Pent-y-bont-fawr, Oswestry, before her death in 1979 she had held the post of official harpist to Charles, Prince of Wales.

In the world of art, Ceri Richards was the Welsh painter and printmaker who, after studying engineering draughtsmanship, studied at Swansea College of Art, now part of Swansea Metropolitan University.

Born in 1903 in the small village of Dunant,

near Swansea, his many works include his 1973 *Still Life with Music* while he also designed the stained glass windows for the Blessed Sacrament Chapel of Liverpool Metropolitan Cathedral and also for Derby Cathedral.

The recipient of a CBE for his artistic contributions, he died in 1971.

In the world of politics, Robert Richards was the Liberal Party politician, historian and antiquarian who served in the early 1920s as Under-Secretary of State for India, while during the Second World War he was head of the civil defence service for North Wales.

Born in 1884 in Tan-y-fford, Llangynog, Montgomeryshire and the author of a number of acclaimed works that include his 1933 *Cymu'r Oeseau Canol*, he died in 1954.

A leading campaigner for the rights of Welsh miners, Thomas Richards was born in Beaufort, Ebbw Vale, Glamorganshire in 1859.

Aged only 12 when he started work in the dank and dangerous depths of the coalmines, he went on to hold a number of posts before his death in 1931 that included president of the Miners Federation of Great Britain and Labour MP for West Monmouthshire.

Bearers of the Richards name have also gained honours and distinction on the field of battle.

Born in 1879, Alfred Richards was a recipient

during the carnage of the First World War of the Victoria Cross (VC), the highest award for gallantry in the face of enemy action for British and Commonwealth forces.

It was in April of 1915, as a sergeant in the 1st Battalion, The Lancashire Fusiliers, that during the Gallipoli campaign he mounted a successful attack on a Turkish machine-gun position.

Severely wounded in the action and having to have a leg amputated, he nevertheless served in the Home Guard during the Second World War; he died in 1952.

Born in Liverpool in 1919, Albert Richards was not only a combatant but also a war artist during the Second World War.

It was after studying at the Royal College of Art that in 1940 he enlisted with the Royal Engineers and, in addition to his military duties, executed paintings of everyday army life in training camps and barracks.

This led to him being appointed to the War Artists' Advisory Committee while, eager for combat, he volunteered as a paratrooper in 1943.

This resulted in paintings such as his iconic *The Drop*, depicting exercises for the D-Day landings of June 1944 and also scenes from the attack on Pegasus Bridge, Arnhem.

Killed in action in May of 1945 when his jeep struck a landmine, his works are today held in collections that include the Imperial War Museum and the Tate.

In contemporary times, General David Richards is the retired British Army officer who served as Chief of the Defence Staff from 2010 to 2013.

Born in 1952 and having served as a major general with NATO, he was elevated to the Peerage in 2004 as Baron Richards of Herstmonceux.

Born in 1958, Vice Admiral Alan Richards is the Royal Navy officer who in 2012 was appointed Chief of Defence Intelligence, while Lieutenant Colonel Anthony Richards has held the post of Equerry to the Queen and Deputy Master of the Royal Household since 1999.

Born in 1953, the many military posts he has held include second in command of the 1st Battalion of the Welsh Guards.

One particularly inventive American bearer of the Richards name was Charles Richards, instrumental in the development of the Colt Single Action Revolver known as the "Peacemaker."

It was along with fellow inventor William Mason that he first developed the iconic firearm in 1873.

Born in 1835 and one of the founding members

of the American Society of Mechanical Engineers, he died in 1919.

From warfare and weapons to decidedly more peaceful pursuits, Ellen Swallow Richards was the American industrial and environmental chemist recognised as having laid the foundations of what is now the science of home economics.

Born in 1842 in Dunstable, Massachusetts, she was the first woman admitted to the prestigious Massachusetts Institute of Technology (MIT), graduating in 1873, while three years earlier she had become the first American woman to earn a degree in chemistry from Vassar College.

A pioneer of work in sanitary engineering and domestic science – laying the basis for home economics – she died in 1911.

An inductee of America's National Women's Hall of Fame, her original home in Dunstable has been designated a National Historic Landmark.

*Chapter four:*

# On the world stage

**An inductee of the Songwriters Hall of Fame, Keith Richards is the legendary English guitarist and singer who is one of the original members of the Rolling Stones.**

Born in 1943 in Dartford, Kent, the son of a factory worker, Welsh blood flows through his veins through his great-grandfather's family, while his maternal grandfather Augustus Dupree toured Britain with his jazz band Gus Dupree and his Boys.

One of his neighbours, with whom he attended Wentworth Primary School, was the future Rolling Stones front-man Mick Jagger and a number of years after the Richards family had moved home, Richards met up with him again by chance on a train.

Richards had first picked up the guitar at an early age and found that both he and Jagger shared an interest in rhythm and blues.

Following their meeting, Richards was persuaded to join the amateur band Little Boy Blue and the Blue Boys, featuring Jagger as its singer, but after the band folded the pair joined with Brian Jones and Scotsman Ian Stewart to form the Rolling Stones.

Having left Sidcup Art College in 1962 and devoting his life to music, Richards shared a flat for a time with Jagger and Jones.

Signed to Decca Records in 1963 and with Stewart having left the band and Charlie Watts and Bill Wyman having joined, their manager Andrew Loog Oldham decided to drop the 's' from Richards' surname, persuading him that "Keith Richard looked more pop."

In the early 1970s, however, Richards reverted back to the original spelling of his surname.

As songwriters, early Jagger and Richards hits included, for Marian Faithfull, *As Tears Go By* and Gene Pitney's recording of their *That Girl Belongs to Yesterday*.

In their own right, the Rolling Stones have gone on to enjoy a string of hits that include *(I Can't Get No) Satisfaction*, *The Last Time*, *Honky Tonk Women*, *Brown Sugar*, *Wild Horses*, *Jumpin' Jack Flash*, and *Start Me Up*.

The subject of a number of arrests for illicit drug use in the 1960s and 1970s, Richards was treated for heroin addiction in the United States in 1977.

An inspiration for actor Johnny Depp's character Captain Jack Sparrow in the *Pirates of the Caribbean* series of films, Richards sustained a head injury after falling from a tree while the 2007 *Pirates of the Caribbean: At World's End*, in which he has a cameo role, was being filmed in Fiji.

Also a successful solo artist, in addition to induction into the Songwriters Hall of Fame in 1993, he is also ranked by *Rolling Stone* magazine at No. 4 in its list of 100 Best Guitarists, while his candid autobiography *Life* was published in 2010.

With the popular Richards spelling variation of 'Richard', Harry Rodger Webb, born to English parents in 1940 in Lucknow, India, is the veteran singer, musician and performer better known as **Cliff Richard**.

His father worked for a catering company that serviced the Indian railways and, following the granting of Indian independence in 1947, the family moved back to England and settled in Surrey.

Expressing an interest in skiffle music, the future best-selling singer's father bought him a guitar when he was aged 16.

This helped to set him on the road to stardom, releasing the first of his many hit singles, *Move It*, in 1958.

He adopted the surname 'Richard' in recognition of his American music idol Little Richard and 'Cliff', as in 'rock-face', suggesting 'rock.'

With the Shadows as his backing group, he enjoyed enormous success throughout the late 1950s and early 1960s, appearing with the band in films that include *The Young Ones* and *Summer Holiday*.

Parting company with the Shadows, who remained a best-selling band in their own right, he became a devout Christian and, in addition to recording hits that include *The Day I Met Marie*, *Miss You Nights*, *We Don't Talk Anymore* and *Devil Woman*, he also recorded gospel music.

Representing the United Kingdom in the 1968 Eurovision Song Contest with *Congratulations*, he was placed second, while five years later he was placed third with *Power to All Our Friends*.

Best known as the lead singer of the British pop group Steps, **Claire Richards** was born in 1977 in Hillingdon, London.

It was while working as a receptionist that in 1997 she auditioned for the line-up that would become the best-selling group – and was offered a place on condition that she lose weight.

Along with Lee Latchford-Evans, Faye Tozer, Lisa Scott-Lee and Ian "H" Watkins, she had answered an advert in *The Stage* magazine placed by the songwriters Steve Crosby and Barry Upton and band manager Tim Byrne.

The band enjoyed a number of hits that include *5,6,7,8*, *Deeper Shade of Blue* and S*ay You'll Be Mine* before Richards decided to leave the band, leading it to split up – much to the dismay of its legions of fans – in 2001.

Richards and her fellow band member Watkins continued as a duo, having chart success with the single *DJ*, while the group reformed in 2011.

In a much different musical genre, **Ann Richards** was the stage name of the American jazz singer Margaret Ann Borden, born in 1935 in San Diego, California.

Beginning her professional career when she was aged 19, she played for Stan Kenton, the band leader whom she later married.

The couple separated in 1961, the same year in which she became the subject of scandal after posing for *Playboy* magazine.

With best-selling albums that include her 1958 *I'm Shooting High*, the troubled singer took her own life in 1982.

In the recording studio, **David Richards**, born in 1956, is the Swiss-based record producer, engineer and musician who has co-produced albums for Queen and David Bowie.

This was at Mountain Studios, owned by

Queen, in Montreux, while he has also produced live music recordings for events that include the Montreux Jazz Festival.

From music to the stage, **Denise Lee Richards** is the American actress and former fashion model who was married from 2002 to 2006 to fellow actor Charlie Sheen.

Born in 1971 in Downers Grove, Illinois, her big screen credits include the 1997 *Starship Troopers* and the 1998 *Wild Things*, while she played the role of nuclear physicist Christmas Jones in the 1999 James Bond film *The World Is Not Enough*.

In the early Richards homeland of Wales, **Erin Richards** is the actress born in 1986 in Penarth, Vale of Glamorgan.

Best known for her role of a detective in the television series *Being Human*, other credits include the series *Gotham*, while she also appears in the 2013 horror film *Open Grave*.

Born in London in 1946, **Gavin Richards** is the British actor of stage and television whose credits include the role from 1987 to 1989 of Captain Alberto Bertorelli in the sitcom *'Allo 'Allo!* and that of Terry Raymond from 1996 to 2002 in the soap *EastEnders*.

Back on American shores, **Kim Richards** is the former child actress born in 1964 in Mineola, New

York, and the star of a number of Disney films that include the 1975 *Escape to Witch Mountain* and the 1976 *No Deposit, No Return*.

Also one of the personalities of the television series *The Real Housewives of Beverley Hills*, she is the older sister of the actress **Kyle Richards**.

Born in 1969 and also a former child actress, appearing in the television series *Little House on the Prairie* and films that include the horror films *The Car* and *Halloween*, she has also appeared with her sister on *The Real Housewives of Beverley Hills*.

Another former child actress is **Ariana Richards**, born in 1979 in Healdsburg, California and whose credits include the 1990 *Tremors* and, from 1993, *Jurassic Park*.

An award-winning actress of stage, television and film, **Beah Richards** was the stage name of Beulah Elizabeth Richardson, born in 1920 in Vicksburg, Mississippi.

Nominated for a Tony Award for her performance in the 1965 Broadway production of *The Amen Corner*, she also received an Academy Award Nomination for Best Supporting Actress for her role of Sidney Poitier's mother in the 1967 film *Guess Who's Coming to Dinner*.

With television credits that include *Benson*,

*The Big Valley* and *The Practice* and the recipient of two Primetime Emmy Awards, she died in 2000.

Born in 1944, **Angela Richards** is the English actress and singer whose television credits include the drama series *Secret Army*, *Minder* and *Hetty Wainthrop Investigates*, while on stage she has played the role of Grizabella in *Cats*.

Behind the camera lens, **Martin Richards** is the award-winning American producer for stage and film whose Broadway production of *Chicago* won a Tony Award for Best Revival of a Musical and three Tony Awards for Best Musical.

Born in 1932, he also won the Academy award for Best Picture for his production of the 2002 film of the name, while other films on which he has worked include the 1978 *The Boys from Brazil* and, from 1981, *The Shining*.

Founder of the New York Center for Children to care for abused children and their families, he died in 2012.

Bearers of the Richards name have also excelled in the highly competitive world of sport.

In the saddle, **Gordon Richards** was the English champion jockey born in 1904 in the village of Donnington Wood, Shropshire, the son of a coal miner.

It was in 1925, six years after becoming a

stable boy in Wiltshire, that he became a professional jockey – becoming Champion Jockey in his first year with 118 wins.

Despite being incapacitated for a time through tuberculosis, he went on to win a series of prestigious events that include the 2,000 Guineas at Newmarket in 1947 aboard Tudor Minstrel and the 1953 Epsom Derby riding Pinza.

British flat racing Champion Jockey for what still stands as a record 26 times, a pelvic injury put an end to his racing career a year after winning the Derby.

Continuing as a trainer and knighted for his services to the sport, he died in 1986, while *Racing Post* has ranked him at No.1 in its list of the top 50 jockeys of the twentieth century.

In the rough and tumble that is the game of rugby, David Richards, better known as **Dai Richards**, is the Welsh former international rugby union player born in 1954 in Cwmgwrach, Neath.

Capped seventeen times for his nation and having toured with the British Lions, he played club rugby for Swansea and has been a national selector for the Welsh Rugby Union.

Born in Nuneaton in 1963, **Dean Richards** is the English former rugby union player who played for both England and the British and Irish Lions.

A former police constable, he played club rugby for Leicester Tigers, while posts he has held since include director of rugby for Harlequins.

Having represented New Zealand at four rugby union world cups, **Anna Richards** is one of her nation's most capped Black Ferns – as the women's national team is known.

Born in 1964 in Timaru, she is also an inductee of the International Rugby Board (IRB) Hall of Fame.

From rugby to athletics, **Robert Eugene Richards** is the American former pole vaulter and decathlete nicknamed the "Pole Vaulting Parson" and the "Vaulting Vicar."

Born in 1926 in Illinois and ordained a minister in the Church of the Brethren in 1946, he won the Olympic Gold Medal for the pole vault in both 1952 and 1956.

The first athlete to appear, in 1958, on the front of *Wheaties* cereal boxes, he is an inductee of the U.S. Olympic Hall of Fame and the United States National Track and Field Hall of Fame.

One particularly intrepid bearer of the proud name of Richards is the British yachtswoman **Emma Richards** who, when she was aged 27, became the youngest person ever to complete the gruelling Around Alone single-handed around the world yacht race.

English-born, she was aged five when her family moved to Scotland where her father had taken up the post of chair of aeronautics and fluid mechanics at Glasgow University.

The family settled in Helensburgh, and the west coast town proved an ideal location for them to indulge their passion for sailing – and by the age of only eleven Emma was competing in dinghy world championships.

Graduating from Glasgow University in 1996 with a degree in sports medicine and a member of the Scottish National Olympic Training Squad, she entered the Around Alone event in 2002 – starting and finishing in America and covering some 28,800 miles of ocean.

After 132 exhausting days, she became the youngest ever, and the first British woman, to complete the challenge.

Awarded an MBE in 2003 in recognition of her impressive feat, she is married to the New Zealand yachtsman Mike "Moose" Sanderson.